LOST LINES OF ENGLAND AND WALES
WYE VALLEY

G. P. ESSEX

GRAFFEG

CONTENTS

FOREWORD

The Wye Valley was a busy industrial area before the railway arrived. The entire Forest of Dean has a long history of industrial activity, due to the abundance of wood for charcoal, iron ore and coal, and the Romans had extensive iron ore mining operations around the forest.

In 1556 a metalworking centre was established at Tintern to produce a fine quality iron wire, primarily for use as carding combs in the rapidly expanding woollen industry. Tintern was also where the first brass was smelted in the UK, in 1568. The River Wye was a busy highway for goods from the area, with flat-bottomed trows carrying coal, wood, charcoal, iron ore and limestone downstream to Bristol and up the Severn to Gloucester.

The area was already recognised for its natural beauty, and John Egerton, a clergyman from Ross On Wye, is credited as developing the idea of modern tourism here. He started taking sightseers on boat trips down the River Wye in 1745 to appreciate the scenery as well as the historical sights. In 1826 a turnpike road was built along the valley and was soon host to carriage tours alongside the river trips.

The Wye Valley Railway Company was formed in 1866 at the end of the last Victorian period of Railway Mania, where numerous schemes had not materialised and many people had lost their speculative investments. The Wye Valley Line was not exempt from the fallout and although it was eventually completed, opening in 1876, it struggled to make money. Operated by the GWR from the beginning, after various boardroom wrangles and two periods in receivership the line was sold to the GWR in 1904.

The line never saw the expected traffic from being an alternate route from south Wales to the Midlands and eventually passenger services were withdrawn in 1959. A limited freight service continued for tinplate from Redbrook and stone from two quarries, with the final services from Tidenham Quarry finally ending in 1992.

INTRODUCTION

This lost line winds its way for 13 miles along the River Wye valley, crossing the English/Welsh border several times, with both termini ending at Welsh junction stations. Although plans for the line emerged in 1865, disagreement over the gauge of the proposed railway between supporters of the GWR broad gauge (7ft 1/4") and the rapidly expanding standard gauge (4ft 8 1/2"), along with financial concerns as the last Railway Mania bubble burst in the late 1860s, meant that construction didn't start until May 1874.

The original proposers had several objectives with the railway: to join the existing railways at Chepstow and Monmouth, to provide a link between the Severn Tunnel, which was then being built, and the Midlands for freight and to obtain a share of the ever-increasing tourist trade along the Wye. Tintern was already established as a tourist destination, and some of the most famous poets, writers and artists of the day visited Goodrich, Tintern and Chepstow. As well as Coleridge, Thackeray and Turner, who painted

Tintern Abbey in 1794, Wordsworth was also inspired, writing 'Lines Written a Few Miles above Tintern Abbey' in 1798.

There was already an early railway in place at Monmouth, known as the Monmouth Tramroad. The Monmouth Railway Company obtained an Act of Parliament in 1810 for building a railway or tramroad from Howler Slade in the Forest of Dean to a terminus at May Hill, near Monmouth. The Act specifically allowed for the conveyance of passengers, thought to be the first to have done so, although there is no evidence that passengers were transported on a regular basis. Opened in 1812, it mainly carried coal and lime from the Forest to Monmouth. From May Hill it ran through Wyesham, Redbrook and Newland to Coleford and on to various collieries and iron mines. Several extensions were added in later years and it reached a total length of almost 9 miles of 3ft 6inch gauge track. Mostly horse-drawn, it had two rope-worked inclines at Poolway and Redbrook, where it descended into the tinplate works (the very steep incline bridge on the Redbrook branch is still in situ). On 4th February 1853, the Coleford, Monmouth, Usk and Pontypool Railway agreed to purchase the Coleford to Monmouth section, but by 1872 there was little traffic. The line was lifted and most of the trackbed was used for the construction of the Great Western Railway's Coleford Branch, which opened on 1st September 1883.

The first plans for the Wye Valley Railway took the route along the western bank of the Wye through Tintern. These plans were revised for several reasons, including the possibility of damage to the ruins of the Abbey, which stood on the western bank, close to the river, a risk that was raised by a House of Lords select committee. Under the revised plans the route now ran along the eastern bank and a proposal was submitted to Parliament in July 1866 and subsequently approved. A share issue for £230,000 was offered to the public in August 1866.

However, construction didn't begin for another eight years, obtaining the necessary finance being the main obstacle. The bubble had burst on the latest Railway Mania investing frenzy in 1866, which resulted in sources of finance drying up. As the original Act of Parliament had a time limit, a new one was required, resulting in the Wye Valley Railway Act of 16th June 1871.

The company appointed S. H. Yockney and Sons of St Anne's Gate, London as engineers for the line and to design and supervise the works. Samuel Hansard Yockney was the senior partner, with his son, Sydney Yockney in the role of junior partner and Resident Engineer. Samuel had come to the attention of Brunel when he was an engineer for the GWR managing the construction of the famous Box Tunnel in Wiltshire, and he went on to manage construction of several other notable works, including Newport and Dudley tunnels and the Sirhowy Tramroad in south Wales.

Construction finally started in May 1874 in Tintern, which is roughly the centre of the line. The contractors, Messrs Reed Bros. & Co. of London, worked in both directions simultaneously and the works included the late addition of the Wireworks Branch. After the original route had been altered, it no longer served the Abbey Wire and Tinplate Company Works, situated between Tintern Abbey and the main village. After protests about the route, the railway company conceded, with an agreement in November 1872 between the Wye Valley Railway Co. and the landowner, the Duke of Beaufort, who also owned the wireworks, that they would construct a branch across the river to serve the Abbey Wireworks.

The construction of the half-mile-long Wireworks Branch included a truss girder bridge over the River Wye, which opened after just two months of construction work in August 1875, three months before the rest of the line. However, the wireworks closed down some weeks before the completion of the branch, which saw little traffic until the Abbey Wire and Tinplate Co. re-opened in the early 1880s, only to finally close for good by 1901. The branch then saw some use by Jones & Son, a sawmill and turnery at Tintern, to carry goods in horse-drawn wagons. By 1935 the track had become unusable and the branch finally closed, with the track being lifted in 1941. Ownership eventually passed to the Gwent and Gloucestershire County Councils, with the bridge providing public access from Tintern to the woods on the Gloucestershire side as part of the Wye Valley Greenway cycling and walking path.

The difficulty of the construction work varied enormously along the route. Sections such as the two miles between Wyesham and Redbook at the Monmouth end of the line were fairly straightforward, and involved cutting a shelf wide enough for the single-track line along the shallow slope of the river valley. This was then formed into a stable and level base with the addition of large pieces of stone – some of these can still be seen along the trackbed.

The more involved sections of line included the two tunnels at Tintern and Tidenham and the viaducts at Redbrook, Shorn Cliff and Monmouth. All of these structures are still in existence today, although the steel truss girder bridge that crossed the River Wye and joined both sections of Monmouth's stone viaduct was removed soon after closure.

The northern terminus, Monmouth Troy, takes its unusual name from the neighbouring Troy House and the River Trothy. Three separate lines terminated here: first was the Coleford, Monmouth, Usk and Pontypool Railway, who built the station in 1857 (their line entered the station from the south through a short tunnel). The line

Monmouth Troy Station

north to Ross On Wye, through Monmouth's other station, May Hill, followed in 1874, with the Wye Valley Railway arriving in 1876. Finally, the short branch to Coleford opened in 1883, sharing the Wye Valley line as far as Wyesham, where it took over the route of the Monmouth Tramway to Newland and Coleford.

The most difficult and expensive section undertaken was the Tidenham Tunnel. At 1,120 yards long, excavated by hand through carboniferous limestone, tunnelling proceeded at around two yards a day and took almost two years to complete. At the time of opening there were two tunnels, separated by a short cutting at Netherhope, the southern end of the tunnel. Between 1900 and 1919 the tunnel was extended by arching over the Netherhope cutting, resulting in a total final length of 1,190 yards.

The line continued south in a cutting before crossing the main A48 Chepstow road on a high embankment that was constructed with a 1 in 66 gradient down to the Wye Valley Junction, where it joined the south Wales to Gloucester main line. The final mile and a quarter journey into Chepstow along the main line included

another crossing of the River Wye, this time over a spectacular tubular bridge built by Brunel. This bridge, which spanned the Wye 50 feet above high tide, by instruction of the Admiralty, was the prototype for Brunel's more famous Royal Albert Bridge over the River Tamar at Saltash, Cornwall. The bridge was built in 1852, cutting journey times between London and south Wales dramatically, at a cost of £77,000 (£11 million today).

The final cost for the single-track line was £318,000 (£47 million today), with the Tidenham tunnel accounting for a large part of that. It also took its toll on the workers, with the *Monmouth Merlin* newspaper reporting the death of 41-year-old Peter Pidsley, a navvy working on the tunnel, who was crushed by a falling rock. Other records show that several men sustained serious injuries during the tunnel construction, but the total number of injuries amongst the several hundred navvies employed for construction is unknown.

As was often the case, the railway saw two openings, the official junket on 21st October 1876 and, almost a fortnight later on 1st November, the start of scheduled services. The *Illustrated London News* reported that the party, numbering around

50 people, included directors of both the Wye Valley Railway Company and the Great Western Railway, as well as numerous local dignitaries. They departed from Chepstow at 12.30 and luncheon was served in Tintern after a tour of the Abbey ruins. The party carried on to Monmouth in the afternoon, where church bells were rung and a grand dinner was served with the usual toasts and speeches.

The line was operated by the Great Western Railway from its opening and leased to them in perpetuity, with the company paying 50% of gross receipts as rental for the line. Despite this advantageous arrangement for the Wye Valley Railway, which received its revenue irrespective of running costs, the company struggled to pay dividends, or even turn a profit. Various issues were cited for the financial troubles: bad weather affecting the tourist trade, locals deterred by poor services, disagreements between the WVR and GWR and the problem of the Wireworks branch. The agreement for building the branch came with the condition that no toll could be charged for that section of line, although the company had to maintain it. The sole income came from the later addition of a weighbridge to the site in 1881,

which gave an annual income to the company of ten shillings.

Further problems arose with mismanagement and irregularities found in financial matters, and in 1881 legal action was taken against members of the board, resulting in the shareholders appointing a receiver. Despite this, the situation grew worse. Various circumstances contributed to the dismal returns, including the closure of the tinplate works at Redbrook, poor services and lack of facilities. In 1882 local residents sent a petition to the GWR calling for improvements.

Despite the receiver and the appointment of a new chairman and board, the railway's poor position continued to worsen, leading to the appointment of a second receiver in 1889 in order to wind up the company's affairs and arrange sale of the line to the GWR. The sale was not immediately forthcoming, as a newly appointed director wrote to shareholders advising them to reject the sale and a unanimous decision could not be reached.

The railway stumbled on throughout the 1890s and in 1904 the chairman, J. H. Whatcoat, wrote to shareholders to persuade them to agree to a sale. The GWR offered 12.5% of the value of preference shares and 2.5% of the value of ordinary shares, which was unanimously accepted.

With the sale completed by July 1905, the GWR set about improvements to services and maintenance issues were rectified. The First World War had a small impact on the line, with some staff killed in the fighting and Tidenham station closed for the last two years of the war in order to free up staff for other locations.

The end of the war saw improved services, including new Sunday trains intended for tourists. The increase in motor traffic, especially commercial services, had an adverse effect on the line, however, and even the introduction of railcar services and the opening of several new halts couldn't stem the slow decline.

The First World War also saw the demise of the Coleford Branch, which finally closed in 1917. The line had opened in 1883 after conversion from the old horse-drawn Monmouth tramroad, worked from its inception by the Great Western Railway. From its junction with the Wye Valley Line at Wyesham, the line climbed some 150m to Coleford on gradients mostly between 1 in 40 and 1 in 67 with several sharp curves, making it known as a difficult line to work. Two stations were built at Newland and Coleford, the latter directly adjacent to, but initially quite separate from, the Severn & Wye Railway's station. Although the main intention was to provide a direct route for iron ore from the Forest to the south Wales steelworks, traffic was never abundant and when the line closed in January 1917, most of the track was soon lifted for the war effort. The line from Whitecliff Quarry to the Seven & Wye line at Coleford remained, used for limestone trains until 1967. Newland station's site was used by the RAF during World War II, with ammunition stored in the tunnels at Redbrook and Newland.

The Great Western decided to add six new halts to improve access to services for locals, beginning with Whitebrook, Llandogo and Brockweir in 1927. More were built at Wyesham and Penallt in 1931; finally, Netherhope was added in 1932. These unstaffed halts were minimalist affairs, with simple wooden platforms, prefabricated corrugated iron shelters and a running in board.

Four to five trains remained running per day, with two on Sundays and a short working from Chepstow to Tintern. These were supplemented by specials, such as the Harvest Moon excursions. These took place on September evenings, with up to 1,300 people arriving to see Tintern Abbey under the harvest moonlight. The station at Tintern was the largest on the line, having been built with the expectation of tourist traffic to the Abbey, and included an island platform with a run-round loop. From around 1935 until the line closed a camping coach was situated in a siding where holidaymakers could rent a converted redundant carriage as holiday accommodation.

Despite its size, some of the facilities at Tintern were basic. Toilets were flushed with well water, which needed to be pumped up to a holding tank on a daily basis. Water for drinking was delivered by train in milk churns every day. Today Tintern is one of the most complete surviving stations, with the platforms and most of the buildings still intact. It now operates as a cafe and tourist centre.

The Second World War had an even greater impact on Britain's railway network than the First, seeing timetables altered and delays become common-place due to the priority given to troop and equipment trains. In addition, over 100,000 railway staff were released for military service. There was a chronic lack of investment and little in the way of repairs and maintenance over the war years and in 1948 the struggling railway companies were nationalised into British Railways.

Although the excursion trains and other specials continued after the war and were joined by pigeon trains, which carried up to 12,000 birds to Monmouth Troy for annual races, revenue from the line continued to decrease and by the 1950s it was losing £20,000 per year (almost £600,000 today). An illustration of the situation comes from an August 1958 edition of the *Western Mail:* 'Only one ticket sold during a day at Monmouth Railway Station recently – and that was a 6$\frac{1}{2}$d one'. The decision to close the line to passenger traffic was taken before Beeching's notorious report, and the last regular passenger train ran on 3rd January 1959. The final passenger train to use the line was a Stephenson Locomotive Society special, on Sunday 4th January 1959. Double-headed by GWR pannier tanks Nos 6412 and 6439 and carrying over 400 passengers in ex-GWR coaching stock, the train stopped for several photo opportunities as it wound its way along the snow-covered valley. After stopping at Monmouth Troy, the train continued on to Ross-On-Wye, a line which was also being closed at the time.

Freight continued for a number of years, with the Tinplate works at Redbrook and other industries needing their goods to be transported. The Redbrook Tinplate Works produced high-quality plate that was exported worldwide and used in tobacco and confectionery tins, with thicker grades used for food canning. It employed 500 people in the late 1940s but, unable to compete with newer production methods, its demise came in 1962 and the line closed to ordinary goods traffic in 1964. Several railtours took place through Tidenham tunnel in the 1970s; one of the last of these, the 'Tintern Totter' in 1978, was hauled by a Class 20 diesel loco.

The two quarries on the line were still in operation, however, at Tintern, just north of Tidenham Tunnel, and Dayhouse, adjacent to Tidenham station. After closure in 1964 the line was operated as a private siding. Tintern quarry had opened in 1931 and a siding was installed for loading wagons with limestone. This was later converted to a run round loop that had hopper facilities for direct loading of wagons.

The station buildings at Tidenham were demolished soon after closure, but the platform was developed into a loading bay for stone from Dayhouse Quarry and a new loop laid in March 1968. The last train to the quarry ran in September 1992.

The line lay derelict for a number of years, with track on the southern end in place until 2019, but the remaining structures are now mostly in private hands. Tintern Station was purchased by Monmouthshire County Council soon after closure and is a popular cafe and heritage centre. Monmouth Troy station building was purchased and moved stone by stone to the Gloucestershire & Warwickshire heritage railway, where it was rebuilt at Winchcombe station.

The Wye Valley Greenway restored and opened part of the line, including the Wireworks bridge, in 2021 as a cycling and walking path from Chepstow to Tintern. Tidenham tunnel has been adapted as a bat sanctuary with low-level lighting for walkers and cyclists to see their way through. The only other remaining station building, St Briavels, is now in private hands.

SEVERN TUNNEL, CHEPSTOW, and MONMOUTH
(Third class only, limited Accommodation)

Miles	Up	a.m	a.m		p.m	p.m		p.m		Mile	Down	a.m	a.m		p.m	p.m		p.m	
		Week Days only										**Week Days only**							
—	Severn Tunnel Jn. ¶ dep	7‡30	10‡3	..	2‡16	5 0	..	7 10		—	Monmouth (Troy) ¶. de	9 10	1150	..	3 55	6 6	..	8 15	..
2¾	Portskewett...........	7‡38	10‡9	..	2‡23	5 7	..	7 16		2	Redbrook-on-Wye ¶.....	9 17	1157	..	4 1	6 13	..	8 22	..
7¾	Chepstow ¶..........	7 55	10 30	..	2 40	5 16	..	7 25		5¾	St. Briavels ¶..........	9 27	12 7	..	4 11	6 23	..	8 32	..
8¾	Tidenham ¶	8 3	10 39	..	2 48	5 24	..	7 33		9	Tintern ¶	9 36	1216	..	4 23	6 33	..	8 42	..
12¾	Tintern ¶	8 14	10 49	..	2 58	5 34	..	7 43		13	Tidenham ¶..........	9 47	1226	..	4 34	6 44	..	8 53	..
16¾	St. Briavels ¶	8 23	11 0	..	3 7	5 42	..	7 52		14½	Chepstow **75**	9 55	1233	..	4 40	6 51	..	9 7	..
19¾	Redbrook-on-Wye ¶...	8 34	11 10	..	3 17	5 52	..	8 3		19	Portskewett ¶.......[69	10‡16	1242	..	4 49	7‡18	..	9 20	..
21¾	Monmouth (Troy) 128 ar	8 43	11 19	..	3 26	6 1	..	8 10		21¾	Severn Tunnel Jn. 64, ar	10‡23	1248	..	4 55	7 3	..	9 28	..

‡ Change at Chepstow.

¶ "Halts" at Caldicot, between Severn Tunnel Junction and Portskewett, at Tutshill (for Beachley), between Chepstow and Tidenham, at Netherhope, between Tidenham and Tintern, at Brockweir and at Llandogo, between Tintern and St. Briavels, at Whitebrook and at Penallt, between St. Briavels and Redbrook-on-Wye, and at Wyesham, between Redbrook-on-Wye and Monmouth (Troy).

OTHER TRAINS between Severn Tunnel Junction and Chepstow, see page 75.

Illustrated above is the Wye Valley Railway timetable for May and June 1947 from *Bradshaw's British Railways Guide*. Note that the individual times for the halts are not included, but their names are added below the table. Bradshaw's Timetables began in 1840 and combined the timetables of up to 150 railway companies in one monthly volume. They continued production until 1961, when the British Railways UK timetable set for the entire network was sold for half the price of Bradshaw's volume.

MONMOUTH TROY

A large crowd has gathered at Monmouth Troy station to watch the coffin of Charles Rolls being unloaded from a train in July 1910. Rolls, the co-founder of Rolls Royce Motors and a pioneer aviator, died aged 32 when his French-built Wright biplane broke up in mid-air. Although only 20ft up, as a result of the fall he became Britain's first powered aircraft fatality. This view of the station, taken from the road above the tunnel portal, was a popular location for many photographers, with the viaduct leading to the River Wye Bridge just visible in the distance. The locomotive at the adjacent platform is an 0-6-0 2301 class known as a 'Dean Goods', after the designer, Great Western locomotive superintendent William Dean.

Monmouth Viaduct
Wyesham Halt
Monmouth Troy
Halfway House
Newland
Coleford
Redbrook
Penallt Halt
Whitebrook Halt
St Briavels
Llandogo Halt
Brockweir Halt
Tintern
Tintern Quarry
Wye Valley Junction
Netherhope Halt
Tidenham
Tutshill Halt
Chepstow Bridge
River Wye Bridge
Chepstow

A trio of passenger services stand at Monmouth Troy station on 1st September 1953. Ex-Great Western diesel railcar No W21 is on the Chepstow service, with classmate No W30 on a Pontypool Road working behind and ex-Great Western 14xx class 0-4-2 at the rear. These railcars, a regular feature on the Wye Valley Line and forerunners of the multiple units used today, were developed by the Great Western Railway in the early 1930s as a viable means of operating small branch lines. With driving cabs at each end and fitted with buffers and couplings, they could have a goods van or another passenger carriage attached to enable them to provide a complete service on branch lines. The Great Western built 38 railcars, with three surviving in preservation.

Ex-Great Western 0-6-0 Pannier tank No 6409 is seen in the Up platform at Monmouth Troy with a Chepstow train on 5th October 1957. The tunnel carrying the lines to Pontypool can be seen in the background. The tunnel portal is still in situ, although bricked up, however, virtually no trace remains of the station itself, the main site being derelict. There was a large goods yard to the north of the station, with six sidings, a ten-ton crane, goods shed and cattle dock. The goods shed was demolished in 1987 and a housing estate now stands on the site of the yard. The station building was hand demolished in 1987 and relocated to Winchcombe Station on the Gloucestershire Warwickshire Steam Railway, being reassembled and in use several years later.

This view of Monmouth Troy shows the diverging lines to Ross On Wye on the left and Chepstow and the Wye Valley on the right. The steel girder bridge on the Ross line can just be seen in the distance. A Great Western 14xx class 0-4-2 tank locomotive waits at the platform with a Wye Valley train.

Note the 'E' on the right-hand end of the box goods wagon in the siding on the left, denoting a London North Eastern Railway wagon. Goods wagons travelled extensively around the UK railway network, often ending up in another railway company's goods yard.

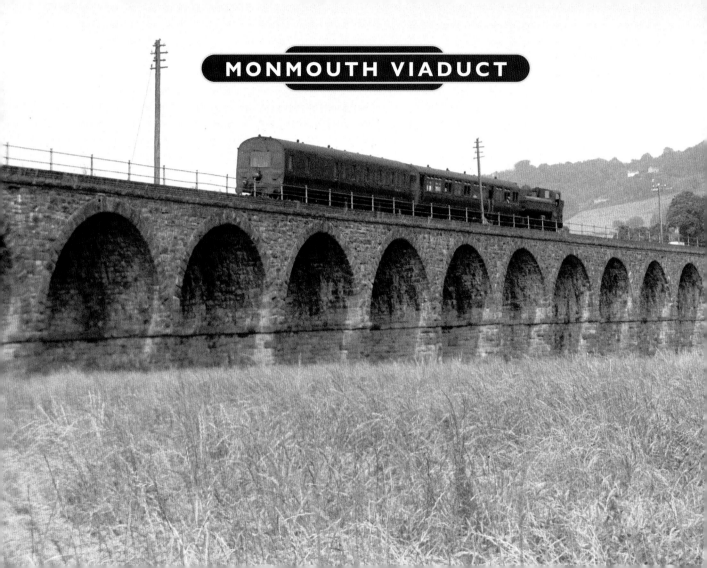

MONMOUTH VIADUCT

An ex-Great Western Pannier tank-hauled autotrain crosses Monmouth viaduct (LC). The viaduct starts at the junction with the Ross on Wye line and crosses the River Wye before curving round to Wyesham Halt. Also known as the Chippenham Meadow viaduct (LC), this 20-arch, 200-yard red sandstone construction had two 75-foot steel lattice-girder spans over the river that were removed shortly after the line closed. Originally designed as a wooden structure, this was changed by the engineers after flooding covered the meadows in 1852. The structure took ten months to build and contains around 9,000 cubic yards of masonry and 3,000 cubic yards of concrete. The stone sections are extant today – it is fenced off at the high level but the riverside path crosses underneath and can be accessed by walking along the trackbed from the former station site.

WYESHAM HALT

A Great Western autotrain at Wyesham Halt heads for Monmouth on an unknown date. This picture shows the basic nature of the halt's construction. Autotrains were a common feature on Great Western branch lines, allowing the driver to operate the locomotive from the end of the carriage without having to 'run round' the train at the end of the line. Inside the small cab was a lever that operated a linkage under the carriage connected to the loco's regulator, a brake valve and a bell system to communicate with the fireman. The large bell seen below the driver's window was operated by a foot pedal and used in place of the loco whistle.

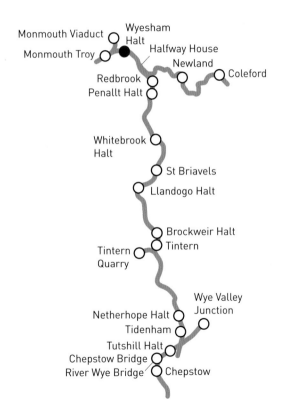

Monmouth Viaduct
Wyesham Halt
Monmouth Troy
Halfway House
Newland
Redbrook
Coleford
Penallt Halt
Whitebrook Halt
St Briavels
Llandogo Halt
Brockweir Halt
Tintern
Tintern Quarry
Wye Valley Junction
Netherhope Halt
Tidenham
Tutshill Halt
Chepstow Bridge
River Wye Bridge
Chepstow

HALFWAY HOUSE

On 16th February 1880 this unfortunate locomotive collided with a large boulder that had landed on the track after a rock fall at a location known as Halfway House, between Wyesham and Redbrook. The loco was hauling a goods train consisting of eight wagons and a brake van. According to the local newspaper, the *Monmouth Merlin*, there were no fatalities, however, the driver, George Beckingham, suffered bruising and severe scalding from the boiler water and the fireman escaped with minor injuries. It seems that the line was opened again quite quickly but that rock falls were a regular feature on some areas of the line, although thankfully no other derailments appear to have occurred.

The locomotive was a Great Western '1016' class 0-6-0 saddle tank, No 1048, designed by Joseph Armstrong and built in 1870 at the Great Western's Stafford Road Works in Wolverhampton. It survived this incident and, once repaired, continued in service until 1930, when it was scrapped.

COLEFORD

A Railway Enthusiasts Club tour entitled 'The Severn Rambler' stops for a photo opportunity and for GWR Pannier tank No 5417 to take on water at Coleford on 20th April 1958. The goods shed that can be seen in the background is the only surviving remnant of Coleford's extensive railway infrastructure. The two adjacent stations of the Wye Valley and Severn & Wye lines have totally vanished beneath car parks and roads, however, the goods shed forms part of the Coleford GWR Museum, which has moved a signal box from near Taunton and the ticket office interior from Monmouth Troy.

Although the station has closed to passengers, as can be seen by the condition of the track, there is some activity in this photo, believed to have been taken in September 1950 during a Birmingham Locomotive Club railtour that visited the Coleford branch along with the Severn & Wye Railway and on to Ross on Wye. Regular traffic from Whitecliff Quarry continued until 1967.

COLEFORD SIGNAL BOX

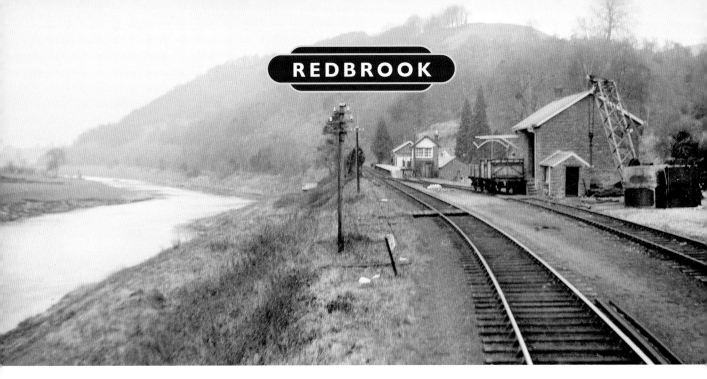

REDBROOK

This view of Redbrook on Wye highlights the station's proximity to the river. The goods shed and yard crane are shown in the foreground, while in the distance the signal box can be seen. Although some freight traffic from the tinplate works continued after passenger services ceased, the works lost business as new, cheaper methods of manufacturing were developed in the nearby south Wales steelworking industry and finally closed in 1962. The station and its associated buildings were demolished in 1964, with a car park and playing field now occupying the site.

Our second view of Redbrook was taken after the line closed, with vegetation taking hold and the running in board having been removed. A sorry sight compared to its heyday, the station won numerous awards for its gardens and their well-maintained flower beds and climbing roses. The signal box, although a sturdily built stone structure, was relegated to part-time use in 1925, when signalling on the line was rationalised, hence the downgrading of the sign from signal box to ground frame. The station also boasted a goods shed, siding and yard crane, which dealt with cargo from the nearby tinplate works.

Penallt Halt, opened in August 1931, was separated from Redbrook station by the short span of Penallt Viaduct, which can be seen in the distance. The viaduct is still in existence, with the footbridge alongside still in regular use. The village of Penallt was famous for producing high-quality millstones from the locally quarried 'pudding stone', an exceptionally hard variety.

WHITEBROOK HALT

Whitebrook Halt is seen from a train on an unknown date, although the corrosion on the base of the corrugated tin shelter suggests that this is a later photo, possibly from the 1950s. All the halts built by the GWR on the line during the late 1920s were of the same design, a standard galvanised shelter supplied by Joseph Ash & Son of Birmingham.

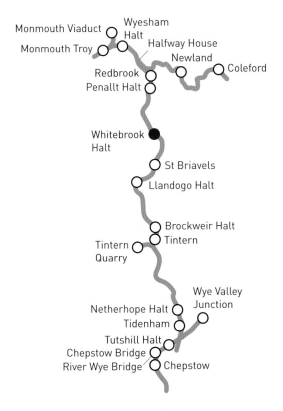

Monmouth Viaduct
Wyesham Halt
Monmouth Troy
Halfway House
Newland
Coleford
Redbrook
Penallt Halt
Whitebrook Halt
St Briavels
Llandogo Halt
Brockweir Halt
Tintern
Tintern Quarry
Netherhope Halt
Wye Valley Junction
Tidenham
Tutshill Halt
Chepstow Bridge
River Wye Bridge
Chepstow

ST BRIAVELS

St Briavels Station viewed from the train, date unknown. This station was renamed three times, opening as Bigsweir after the adjacent River Wye bridge and later becoming St Briavels and Llandogo in 1909 before settling with St Briavels in 1927, when the new Llandogo halt was opened. Out of shot on the right is the goods yard, which consisted of a goods shed, two sidings and two yard cranes. Just ahead of the train are the signal box and level crossing. The station building and platform have survived, now owned by a private fishing club.

BROCKWEIR HALT

Ex-Great Western 64xx class Pannier tank No 6426 arrives at Brockweir Halt with a Monmouth to Chepstow autotrain on Saturday 18th October 1958, less than a year before the line closed to passenger traffic. Built in 1935, this locomotive was based in Newport for much of its working life before being scrapped in 1961. These two-carriage autotrains were frequently seen operating the passenger services on the line, although records show that they often carried barely enough passengers to fill one carriage. The River Wye can clearly be seen just behind the track, and the proximity to the river did cause some problems, with the lower-lying Monmouth end of the line suffering from flooding on several occasions.

On the page opposite, the train seen arriving at Brockweir Halt in the previous picture, headed by No 6426, continues on its way to Chepstow.

This request stop halt was opened in September 1929, on the north side of Brockweir road bridge. Brockweir village was originally served by Tintern station, despite being over half a mile away. There was a convenient direct interchange with the competing Red and White bus service by means of a bus stop at the top of the approach path. The basic wooden platform construction included a surface composed of cinder and ash, which would have been in plentiful supply from the line's locomotives. Though classed as hazardous material today, this was a common surfacing material on many small stations and halts of the period.

TINTERN

The station building at Tintern looks north towards Brockweir halt, a short distance around the curve. The substantial station building still survives, along with the platforms and signal box, although the trackbed has been filled in to provide a picnic area for the station cafe. The former siding and cattle dock now houses two ex-British Rail carriages with a permanent exhibition about the history of the line. The area is now much more heavily wooded and the view across to the houses on the opposite side of the valley is obscured by trees. Railways kept their linesides clear of vegetation in the days of steam due to the risk of fires caused by hot sparks from the locomotives.

This undated view of Tintern shows a typical autotrain on platform 1 heading to Monmouth. The island platform arrangement with three platforms made it the largest station complex on the line. It was anticipated that tourist traffic to visit the world-famous Abbey would warrant the facilities, but despite regular 'Abbey Excursions' it was never as busy as expected. The twin running lines through the station, with the extra loop on the Down side, allowed for short working – trains starting and terminating at Tintern instead of running the full length of the line – which was ideal for the excursion traffic. The goods yard facilities included a set of cattle pens and loading dock, goods shed and sidings. The goods shed has been demolished, but the cattle dock remains in situ.

The last day of passenger services, 4th January 1959, sees a Stephenson Locomotive Society special train being hauled by two former Great Western Pannier tanks, Nos 6412 and 6439, one at each end of the train. The Monmouth Troy to Ross line closed on the same day, with the special service covering both the lines. This photo, taken at Tintern, shows the more relaxed attitude to trespass on the railway at the time; in fact, numerous photos of this special service show passengers and onlookers frequently standing on the tracks. The water tower on the right of the picture is still standing and the platform is still in existence, although the line where this train is standing has been infilled to create a picnic area for the station cafe. The island platform canopy has long since been removed.

TINTERN QUARRY

On 5th May 1971 a British Railways Western Region Type 3 diesel hydraulic locomotive, No D7094, shunts wagons at Tintern Quarry, which had opened in 1931. A siding with loading facilities for hopper wagons can be seen on the right. A small ground frame operated the points into the siding. After the line closed to passenger traffic the quarry traffic continued, with the line to the quarries being operated as a private siding from 1964. The site of the quarry can still clearly be seen today, with a buffer stop and the retaining wall in situ.

NETHERHOPE HALT

The last halt to be built on the line, a short distance north of Tidenham Quarry, Netherhope Halt opened in July 1932. This view shows the entrance to Tidenham Tunnel, just past the Netherhope Lane road bridge. The corrugated iron platform shelter was supplied by Joseph Ash & Son of Birmingham, who provided the Great Western Railway with various prefabricated lineside structures, including water towers and lamp rooms, as well as these platform shelters. The halt was demolished soon after closure and nothing remains on the site.

TIDENHAM

Ex-Great Western 64xx Pannier tank No 6412 is seen at Tidenham, the unkempt appearance of the station suggesting that this was shortly before closure. The locomotive, built at Swindon in 1934, was transferred to Newport shed in 1956 and withdrawn in 1964. Purchased for preservation straight from service with the Western Region of British Railways, it was restored at Buckfastleigh and hauled the first train to run on what is today the South Devon Railway. She also saw a few years of fame whilst starring in *The Flockton Flyer*, a 1970s children's programme on ITV about the reopening of a preserved railway. The station buildings were demolished soon after closure, the site taken over as a loading bay for the adjacent quarry, which continued to operate rail traffic until September 1992.

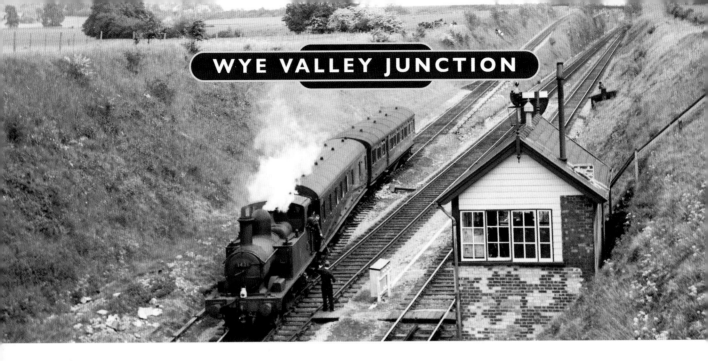

WYE VALLEY JUNCTION

Ex-GWR 14xx class 0-4-2 tank locomotive No 1421 crosses the main line at Wye Valley Junction on the way to Chepstow. The steep 1 in 66 gradient to Tidenham can clearly be seen behind the train. The fireman and signaller are shown exchanging a train staff, as signalling system that existed at that time on much of the UK railway network operated on a block and token system, with trains only being allowed into a section of line – or block – if in possession of a token or staff that the train crew obtained from the signaller at the start of that section. The Wye Valley line consisted of six blocks during the early years of the 20th century, being streamlined over the inter-war years after the closure of the Coleford branch in 1917, resulting in just two blocks by 1927, Monmouth to Tintern and Tintern to Wye Valley Junction. The fireman is shown handing the signaller the staff for the section to Tintern.

On 5th May 1971 a British Railways Western Region Type 3 diesel hydraulic locomotive D7094 is hauling a ballast train on to the main line at Wye Valley Junction. These locomotives, known as 'Hymeks', were built in the early 1960s by the Western Region of British Railways at Swindon Works, who favoured hydraulic transmission systems over the more common diesel electric versions being built by other BR workshops. The non-standard designs and some reliability issues resulted in them being withdrawn after less than 15 years service, with all the class removed from service by 1975. Of the 100 locomotives built, only four remain in preservation today.

TUTSHILL HALT

Ex-GWR 14xx class 0-4-2 tank locomotive No 1421 pulling into Tutshill Halt on 21st May 1958. This locomotive, built in 1933, served most of its 30-year lifespan on various south Wales lines but moved in the 1960s to Reading, Exeter and finally Gloucester before being scrapped in 1964. It was known as Tutshill For Beachley, as can just be seen on the running in board, Beachley being a village on a small peninsula between the mouth of the River Wye and the River Severn. Although the halt was on the main line between Chepstow and Gloucester, passengers had to change at Chepstow to reach the station, as it was only served by Wye Valley line trains.

The basic nature of the wooden platform halts can be seen here, a small corrugated iron shelter is just visible on the closest platform and electric lights on tall concrete posts are now installed. The halt closed, along with the rest of the line, in 1959.

The River Wye bridge at Chepstow viewed from the riverbank, 7th August 1970. This picture shows the rebuilt version of the original 1852 Brunel bridge, on which work was completed in 1962.

CHEPSTOW BRIDGE

Great Western Hall class locomotive No 5927 *Guild Hall* crosses Chepstow Bridge with a southbound passenger train. The loco, one of over 250 Hall class constructed by the GWR, was built in 1933 and spent most of its working life based at Tyseley depot in Birmingham, eventually being scrapped in 1965. This photo shows the original structure of the Brunel-designed bridge, built in 1852. There were limited options for the bridge design due to the geography, with a limestone cliff on one side and low-lying sedimentary ground that was subject to flooding on the other.

Additionally, the Admiralty insisted on adequate clearance for vessels passing underneath. The tubular box girder design was revolutionary and served as a prototype for Brunel's famous Saltash bridge over the River Tamar between Devon and Cornwall. In the 1950s some stress cracking was discovered and the bridge was extensively rebuilt, although it is still supported on Brunel's original pillars. A small cross section of the original tubular girder section is preserved nearby outside the former headquarters of Mabey Bridge Works in Mabey Drive.

CHEPSTOW

Former Great Western 0-4-2 tank loco No 1421 at Chepstow Station with a train for the Wye Valley Line. Note the clear indication to change for the Wye Valley Line on the station sign. The station was built in 1850 for the South Wales Railway by Brunel, although one of his staff, W. Lancaster Owen, carried out the design. He later became the Great Western Railway's district engineer and supervised the raising of the station building in 1877. The station is still in use on the main Newport to Gloucester line, with the footbridge and station building still in situ. Sadly, the matching building on platform two was demolished by British Rail in 1964. The footbridge, which is now Grade II listed, recently underwent strengthening and restoration works.

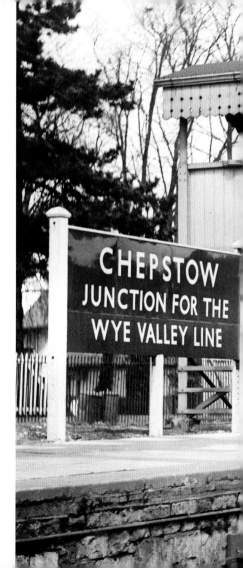

This group of workers are standing in front of the station building at Chepstow whilst in the process of raising it 22 inches in February 1877. The platform at Chepstow was almost 3 feet lower than the train after the south Wales to Gloucester line was converted from Brunel's broad gauge to standard gauge in 1872. This had resulted in numerous complaints about women being unceremoniously bundled onto the train by helpful guards. A Chepstow contractor, Cuthbert William Whalley, undertook the work, which was a new and bold project, for although complete wooden buildings were regularly being lifted and moved in America, raising a stone building was something that had never been attempted.

The building, with an estimated weight of around 200 tons, was internally braced and its doors and windows strapped shut, and then supported with large timbers. The workers, using more than 40 screw jacks, slowly raised it over a period of two days, with the platform being built up underneath.

This view of Chepstow, looking south from the footbridge, is believed to have been taken in the 1930s. The twin-track goods shed can be seen on the right, with a somewhat unusual double-storey office building sticking out between the two lines. With goods traffic diminishing after World War II, later photos show that the inner line had become disused by the late 1950s. The goods shed has survived and now forms part of a builder's merchant's on the goods yard site. The signal box no longer survives, with signalling controlled from Newport. Chepstow saw extensive goods traffic, partly due to the National Shipyard that existed out of shot on the left of the photo. The shipbuilding industry existed in Chepstow until 1966, when the site was sold to Mabey Bridge Building, who provided steelwork for the Severn Bridge. It is now being developed for housing.

CREDITS

Lost Lines of England and Wales – Wye Valley. Published in Great Britain in 2022 by Graffeg Limited.

Written by G. P. Essex copyright © 2022. Designed and produced by Graffeg Limited copyright © 2022.

Graffeg Limited, 24 Stradey Park Business Centre, Mwrwg Road, Llangennech, Llanelli, Carmarthenshire, SA14 8YP, Wales, UK. Tel 01554 824000. www.graffeg.com.

G. P. Essex is hereby identified as the author of this work in accordance with section 77 of the Copyright, Designs and Patents Act 1988.

A CIP Catalogue record for this book is available from the British Library.

ISBN 9781802582017

1 2 3 4 5 6 7 8 9

Printed in China TT120722

G. P. Essex is a writer and photographer specialising in railways. His website can be found at www.randomrailways.com.

Photo credits
© Colour Rail: page 55.
© S.Rickard/J&J Collection: pages 36, 45, 50, 52.
© G. P. Essex: page 13.
© Michael Hale/Great Western Trust: pages 23, 29, 30, 39, 42, 48, 49.
© John Alsop: pages 15, 19, 62.
© Kidderminster Railway Museum: pages 7, 17, 18, 28, 31, 46, 51, 54.
© Lens of Sutton: cover, pages 27, 59.
© thetransportlibrary.co.uk: pages 25, 33, 35, 41.
© Monmouthshire Museums: page 60.

The photographs used in this book have come from a variety of sources. Wherever possible contributors have been identified although some images may have been used without credit or acknowledgement and if this is the case apologies are offered and full credit will be given in any future edition.

Cover: Chepstow.
Back cover: Redbrook, Brockweir Halt, Monmouth Viaduct.

Lost Lines of England:
The Cheddar Valley Line ISBN 9781913134402
Birmingham to Oxford ISBN 9781912654871
Ryde to Cowes ISBN 9781912654864
Stratford-upon-Avon to Gloucester ISBN 9781802582024

Lost Lines of England and Wales:
Shrewsbury to Chester ISBN 9781914079122
Wye Valley ISBN 9781802582017

Lost Lines of Wales series:
Cambrian Coast Line ISBN 9781909823204
Aberystwyth to Carmarthen ISBN 9781909823198
Brecon to Newport ISBN 9781909823181
Ruabon to Barmouth ISBN 9781909823174
Chester to Holyhead ISBN 9781912050697
Shrewsbury to Aberystwyth ISBN 9781912050680
The Mid Wales Line ISBN 9781912050673
Vale of Neath ISBN 9781912050666
Rhyl to Corwen ISBN 9781912213108
Bangor to Afon Wen ISBN 9781912213115
The Heads of the Valleys Line ISBN 9781912654154
Conwy Valley Line ISBN 9781912654147
Llandovery to Craven Arms ISBN 9781914079115
Swansea to Llandovery ISBN 9781914079108
Monmouthshire Eastern Valley ISBN 9781802581089
Monmouthshire Western Valley ISBN 9781802581102